The Black Hat Step By Step Guide To List Building

A R Hipkins

ISBN: **1496144678**
ISBN-13: **978-1496144676**

The Black Hat Step By Step Guide To List Building

CONTENTS

Introduction

As a new Internet marketer, you may have heard that the key to your moneymaking success lies in your list—and this is the truth. In order for any Internet marketer to be truly successful in running his or her online business, they first need to build an extensive list of contacts.

These contacts may not always be first-time customers, but building relationships with them is critical.

Why? One of the largest expenses for businesses is drawing in customers and turning them into sales.

It takes time, effort, and money to draw in your customers, have them purchase an item from you, and never come back. If the customer comes in, but doesn't buy anything, then it's a hit to your bottom line.

Building a list allows you to collect a large number of people with minimal effort, so you can sell to the same people repeatedly.

Building a list establishes relationships, so you can reach out to your subscribers again and again, until they convert into paying, and hopefully returning customers.

As a new Internet marketer, the most important thing you need to learn is that you *must* build a list. While there are several parts to building a successful online business, your list is the single most important aspect, as it is a major driver of income—and what makes money for you while you sleep.

The idea is that once you have your list built, you can send out an email the list promoting a new product or service, and see sales shortly after. You can literally make money in your sleep by adding the promotional emails into an auto-responder series. An auto-responder automatically sends out emails to subscribers at predetermined intervals based on their initial sign up date.

As a marketer, you have the option to create and sell your own products, or to work as an affiliate for other products. There are pros and cons to both approaches. As someone who creates their own products, you have the option to really search the market and the competition and offer something you know will be valuable. However, this means you will have to invest time, effort, and possibly money into the product creation.

As someone who is an affiliate for other products, you will be competition with other affiliates, and you will only get a portion of the sales price. No matter which path you choose, the list is still an integral part of your success.

Setting up your auto-responders will take a bit of time and effort in the beginning, but once they're finished, you can leave them on autopilot.

As long as you check from time to time to make sure your links are still working, you're good to go.

Now that you understand the importance of building an email list, let's get on to the practical action steps you need to take to get it running for your business.

We'll start with creating the opt-in offer's bait, and then move on to the steps for creating your list and setting everything up online.

Subscriber Opt-In Offers

It is important to acknowledge that you should have *something* of value to your target audience to provide to them for free, in exchange for subscribing to your list.

Otherwise, they won't have incentive to do so in the first place, and you will have a hard time building your list. This can be some as simple as a short e-book, or a recording, or a video that relates to your product or service, and helps the user to solve a problem.

Creating Your Opt-In Offer a.k.a. Bait

While this stage will take some time, just like setting up the list and autoresponder emails, it is also something you can "set and forget" and check on periodically to make sure the information is current and all links are functional.

I call this your "bait" because essentially, that's what it is. You're baiting people into subscribing to your list, with something of value to them, in hopes that they will become a paying customer later.

Here are a few options for bait:
☐ ☐ Ebook
☐ ☐ Video/Audio recording
☐ ☐ Short course to teach something of value your readers are interested in
☐ ☐ A periodic newsletter filled with important and pertinent informationfor your readers.

Here's the thing about bait that you need to remember: while you're giving it away for free, it has to be worthy of being paid for. It has to be good.

If your readers don't find it valuable, then they have no reason to stick around—and they *can* unsubscribe at any time.

People are constantly flooded with junk email, so these days they tend to be incredibly careful of who they provide their email address to.

The fact that they're considering opting in to receive your emails is a good sign that they find you trustworthy, and you need to treat them with respect by giving them something that they're not going to get anywhere else.

If you don't grasp this and do well with it, you're shooting yourself in the foot, because this is a key component to your success with Internet marketing, because it is critical to the success of your list building.

Your opt-in offer needs to be good to not only entice people to join the list, but to keep them on it. It needs to: capture their attention, convince them that they want/need it, look appealing, be easy to obtain, and deliver on its promise.

If you're worried about looks, don't worry—we'll be covering that shortly!

To Create or Not Create: That is the Question

At this stage, you have a few options. You can create your opt-in offer yourself, or pay to have it outsourced. Depending on your skills and budget,it may be best to outsource it.

There are plenty of people out there willing to help you! Freelancers are available for hire through a variety of marketplaces such as:
- ☐ ☐ Warrior Forum
- ☐ ☐ oDesk
- ☐ ☐ Elance

You could also source a private label rights product, or PLR and make changes to it to make it your own.

It needs to at least look unique, because if there are other marketers out there promoting the same product, you suddenly lose your edge and appeal. You don't have to do much to it—just changing the name, cover, and a bit of the content works.

How to Choose Your Topic

This topic is crucial because it is part of what will entice people to subscribe to your list.

To determine your topic, you need to ask yourself: "What does my target audience want to know?"

If you are able to determine what people want to know and can then provide them with this information for free, then you've successfully found your bait.

So, how then, do you find what people in your niche really want to know?

It's easier than you think! Do a little bit of detective work in the right places,and you'll get your answer.

Blogs

Using a search engine or blog search engine to find blogs in your niche is a great way to determine how popular a particular topic is.

You can gauge how well people will respond to something based on the number of comments a blog or post receives. It is important to look through popular blogs, because the less popular ones may skew your results, simply because they do not have a large or responsive readership. When you find a post with a lot of comments, it resonated with the audience, whether they responded positively or negatively.

A R Hipkins

Forums

Forums are an excellent way to find people in your niche and see what they're talking about. When you become active in the forums where your customers are, you can build relationships, and you can get a first hand glimpse at what they need, which means you can find or create a product that will help them.

The key is to look and see what questions are asked repeatedly, and to find the biggest problem people are having, and then solve it for them.

If you don't have any idea where your customers are, turn to Google or another search engine of your choice, and search for "your niche + forum" and you'll find the most popular places where your target audience may be hiding.

For example, if you're in the dog-training niche, a popular forum for this group is http://dogforums.com.

Just a few minutes there and you'll find that a lot of people are looking for advice about house breaking, and crate training. This could be a potential bait option for you.

I advise you to look around for a couple hours, and generate a running list of ideas to work with.

Clickbank

Go to http://clickbank.com in your favourite browser, and look for "Marketplace." From there, find your niche take a look at the various products already available for sale. Use this as research, because the popular ones indicate that's what people are buying—because they want to know more about it.

When you do your research, remember you shouldn't steal or copy from these items, but there is nothing wrong with taking the same basic idea and offering your perspective on it to create a unique product for your audience.

For example, let's say you're in the diet and nutrition industry. If we go to Clickbank, we'll see the best selling product is an eBook called "100 Ways to Wellness." By creating something that's similar but unique, you are able to capitalize on something people are already willing to pay for, and by giving it away for free, you can just about guarantee people will come for it—so it's a good option for your list opt-in.

Once you've settled on your topic, you need to stick to it! Changing course in the middle of your game can create a lot of frustration and potentially wasted effort. From here, you will either create the product from scratch, or find a PLR or master reseller rights product.

Building the Squeeze Page

Your squeeze page is one of the most important part of your list building efforts because it is the simple one page website that is designed to "sell" your opt-in offer and get people to join your list.

The site showcases the product you're giving away, while also offering a place for the user to subscribe to get it.

Squeeze Page Examples

Most squeeze pages follow the same basic template, so it makes it easier for you as a marketer, and the customer is typically familiar with them.

Here is an example of squeeze page that's out there and converting well.

DOUBLE YOUR DATING | *ATTRACTION ISN'T A CHOICE*

ATTRACTION MEETING WOMEN DATING TIPS CONFIDENCE GET A GIRLFRIEND PROGRAM CATALOG ABOUT DAVID DEANGELO

Learn Secrets Most Men Will Never Know About Women and Dating

In my FREE Dating Tips Newsletter, You'll Learn:

- How to attract BEAUTIFUL women and stand out from the competition
- An easy, effective way to tell if she's ready to be kissed so you won't get rejected
- Secrets to naturally approaching women, starting conversations and getting dates
- How to get over your fear of rejection - no matter how unsuccessful you've been in the past
- Flirting tips using eye contact and body language
- The secrets of Cocky Comedy - and exactly what to say and do to spark her interest

Master Dating And Attraction Skills That Will Make You Rejection-Proof

Sign up for FREE membership and receive:

- Exclusive Report: "The 10 Most Dangerous Mistakes Men Make With Women"
- Techniques and word for word scripts to create lasting attraction
- Articles and newsletters to help you date the kind of **women you've always wanted**

First Name:

Email:

Dating Success Starts HERE

No Spam Policy | We will not sell your info
Newsletter FAQ | Cancel Newsletter Any Time

Contact Us | Privacy Policy | Terms & Conditions

What Makes for a Good Squeeze Page?

As you can see, we have three different yet effective squeeze pages. They all vary just a little bit—using a combination of text, video, and graphics, to appeal to their audience.

Some will be short, and some will outline with bullet points everything you can expect to learn from the product they're giving away. If you're wondering which of these options works best, unfortunately, there's not an answer.

What works well for one market or niche may not work well for another. It depends on a variety of factors, including how much traffic you're getting, the niche, and the product itself.

If you're just starting out, I recommend using graphic elements, because the graphics will do most of the selling for you, and the copy won't have to be as good in terms of quality.

However, if you are an excellent copywriter, then you can rely a bit more heavily on just copy.

Elements of a Squeeze Page

Your squeeze page will have several different elements:

☐☐**Headline**.
Your headline needs to grab attention while also describing the main thing your readers will learn from the product. For example,
 "Discover the Hidden Health Secrets that Lead to Effortless Weight Loss!" is an option for a weight loss product.

☐☐**Bulleted List.**
The bullet points will provide a bit more information about what your readers will find in the download when they start to read it.
You should keep these short and stick to four or five. Don't give too much information away!

☐☐**Subscription Box.**
Without this, people won't be able to subscribe to your mailing list. You have two options here. You can simply ask for the person's email address, or you can ask for the person's name and email address.
Asking for the name will enable you to add a personalized touch to the email, which like we've said before is key to relationship building.

□□**Submit Button.**

This is the button people click to submit their information and join your list—for the first opt-in. Though they will have to confirm again to actually be subscribed, this is an important part of your squeeze page.

While you can leave the default "submit" button, changing the text to read something like, "Click Here to Continue" or "Click for Instant Access" will increase your opt-in rate.

□□**Privacy statement.**

To put your customers at ease, you should consider adding a line to the squeeze page that tells people you will keep their information confidential.

Otherwise, they may be afraid that you'll sell their email address and leave them victim to floods of spam.

Something simple such as: "Your privacy is important to me,and you'll never have to worry about your information being sold,rented, or given to anyone else, because I, like you, hate spam!"

A R Hipkins

If you need a little help getting started, there are several squeeze page templates online—and if you're using the popular WordPress platform,there are several plugins out there that can help you:

☐ ☐http://landingpagedesigns.net/squeeze-page-templates.html (these

are not free, but they are low cost.)

☐ ☐http://cashrevelations.com/magazine/2010/06/landing-pagetemplates/

(this one offers 150 different options!)

☐ ☐http://landingpagewp.com/ (this will show you a few WordPress options.

Selecting an Auto-responder Email Service

The first key step to setting up a successful auto responder series for an effective list building campaign is to choose the right auto-responder service.

This service will allow you to implement the option to subscribe,while collecting and storing all the subscriber's information (name, email,address) to automate the email series you setup.

While there are free services available, the exchange for a free service means you won't have access to many of the features available in paid services. Some free services may also limit the number of subscribers you can have on your list—and therefore limits your earning potential.

There's also the possibility that a free service can be shut down without warning,which means you lose everything!

Paid services also have additional features so you can track how many subscribers click your links, which in turn helps you see how effective the campaign is.

The most popular providers are Aweber and Get Response. Each of them has pros and cons.

While there are others out there, and you are free to use whatever you want and whatever you feel works best for you—we're going to use Aweber to demonstrate what you need to do, because that's the provider I use.

After selecting your provider, sign up for your account. When you've got your account setup, come back to this book to finish walking through the steps.

Create Your List

If you're using Aweber, these instructions will work exactly as listed. If you're using another provider, they may be slightly different.

Login to your account, and click "Create a New List."

You will then be asked to provide some standard information about your list. Once you fill this out, move on to the "Personalize Your List" screen and make the changes you want.

The one thing of note here is to make sure you name your list something that's easy for you to recognize.

As you make your way into the world of Internet marketing, you will have multiple lists, and making sure they are each distinct will make your job easier in the long run.

At this point, you'll move to the "Confirmed Opt-In Screen" which gives you the option to edit the email your subscribers receive after the subscribe to your list.

All this email does is ask subscribers to confirm all their information to make sure it's correct. This email is sent out as part of the "Double Opt-In"email marketing. While you can turn off the double opt-in as favor of "Single Opt-In" that will negate the email I recommend you keep the double in place.

This helps protect you from SPAM complaints, because the double opt in ensures the user meant to subscribe to your list, and will help you see who the non-responsive subscribers are.

Since the main point of this email list is to build relationships to create customers, I always recommend you edit the emails to add a personal touch
to them. There are several different ways you can do this, but as an example, here's the default email:

Subject: Confirm your subscription.
We received your request for information from the LIST NAME
group. Before we begin sending you the information you requested, we want to be certain we have your permission.
--
CONFIRM BY VISITING THE LINK BELOW:
http://www.aweber.com/z/c/?xxxxxxxx
Click the link above to give us permission to send you information. It's fast and easy! If you cannot click the full URL above, please copy and paste it into your web browser.
--
If you do not want to confirm, simply ignore this message.

Here's how I would change that email to make it a bit more personal for your subscriber:

Hey [name]!
Thanks for requesting my [name of product] report.
Before I send it to you though, I want to be sure you
meant to ask for it. I'm not a big fan of unsolicited email,
and I'm won't send any! Once you click on the link
below,
I'll know you really want my report, and you'll be taken
to the download
page.
[confirmation link]
Thanks!
[your name]

Now you'll be taken to the "Success Page" where you will fill in your download URL, to provide subscribers with the download link to their free opt-in offer.
If you don't have this page of your website setup yet, it's not a big deal.

You can move on with the rest of the report, but you make sure you go back to edit it when you're finished! Now you're ready to add your auto-responder email messages to the system! Click "Messages" and then "Add a New Message".

This message is the first message your subscribers will receive after they've successful opted in and received your free report/download.

The on-screen instructions will guide you through how to do this. To help get you started, here's a sample first email for you to edit. Feel free to edit to suite your needs.

Hi [name]!
Thanks for grabbing my [name of product] report.
In case you haven't gotten it yet, here's the download link again.
[product download URL goes here]
Take some time to read it and let the information soak in. I'm sure you'll enjoy it, and I hope you learn something new! Keep an eye on your inbox for more great tips, tricks and other information from me, because there's a whole lot more where that came from. :)
If you've got any comments, questions, or concerns, drop me a line. I love to hear from my readers, and am here to help in any way I can!
Talk to you soon,
[your name]

From here, you can use the "Messages" tab to include as many follow up messages as you'd like. When you create a new message, be sure to set the interval, or the number of days between the previous message, you'd like to leave before sending the new message.

The number of follow up emails and the space between them will vary depending on your niche, your target audience, and your overall strategy.

Some of you will create daily messages for a short "course" while others may only send a message out every week or so for a limited amount of time.

Getting Down to Business:
How to Insert the Opt-In Form

With your freebie in hand, your list setup with your email marketing manager, and your squeeze page almost complete, now it's time to insert the opt-in page code from Aweber (or another provider) into the squeeze page.

Remember, these instructions are for Aweber users, but other programs will be similar.
1. Login to Aweber, and select the correct list.
2. Click "Web Forms" at the top of the screen.
3. Click "Create New Web Form."
4. Follow the on screen instructions to build your opt-in form.

Important Things to Remember

☐ ☐If possible, have a field for both first name and email. There are some people who say not having a name field helps more people sign up,but many people believe this is not worth the expense of not being able to personalize the emails you send.

☐ ☐Don't forget to change the submit button text.

☐ ☐Make sure the form template matches the design of the squeeze page itself.

☐ ☐Don't forget to add your privacy statement.

When you are happy with your form, you can move on to the next step,which involves the "Settings" page.

Look for the "Thank You Page" box, and choose the "Custom Page" option.In this box, put the URL for your "one time offer" otherwise known as the "upsell" page. When you're happy with this, click "Publish, and then select the "I will publish my form" option. "

Now you'll get a code that looks somewhat intimidating, but you'll need to copy this code and paste it into the location on your squeeze page where you want the box to appear.

Your code will look something like this:

Recommended

- If you change your form here, you won't have to update your website.
- Track statistics in your account.

You can paste the snippet below anywhere between the body tags of your website:

```
<script type="text/javascript" src="http://forms.aweber.com/form/58/817416158.js"></script>
```

A R Hipkins

Building Your One Time Offer/Upsell Page

This step allows you to monetize the list building process, for more power behind your online business.

While the point of this list is to build relationships and create long-term repeat customers, this can help you earn money while you do it, and won't hurt anything.

Some people will disagree with trying to sell something as soon as people subscribe, but I personally have seen success with it and recommend it.

Why? Well, if you think about it, when people subscribe to your list, they are all about *you* at the moment.

They've found your product through your squeeze page, and they've taken the time to provide you with the information to get the freebie—which means they are passionate about whatever it is you're giving them.

By passing you their information, it's a sign they trust you and would more than likely be willing to make a purchase from you.

By grabbing them right at sign up, you should be able to generate some quick income.

A R Hipkins

In fact, if you've been online for any amount of time—
and the fact that you're here tells me you have been—
you've likely seen many of these yourself.

After you subscribe to a mailing list, you've likely seen
some sort of one-time special offers—and whether
you've taken it or not, you should be offering one, too.

It can be a product discount, or a product bundle.
To make this work for you, whatever your special offer is
needs to be closely related to your freebie. Continuing
with our health example from above, let's say you sell
health supplements and vitamins to help with weight loss.

You can offer a free trial bottle, or a discount on their
first bottle.If you don't have your own product to offer,
you could run an affiliate deal and work with the owner
to create a unique deal exclusive to your subscribers.

Many people are more than willing to do this for you
provided you could send them plenty of traffic—because
they're doing the same thing you are!

Building Your Download Page

This is the page people will go to get their freebie, after they've opted-in and confirmed and are officially on the list.

You'll enter the URL to this page on the "Success Page" we talked about before. Don't remember it? Scroll up and see the "Create Your List" section.

It's also a good idea to put the URL to this page in the first auto-responder email—the first one they get after they join—just in case they miss it the first time.

Your download page doesn't have to be fancy. In fact something simple like this would work.

You can also put another related offer on this page if you wanted to.When all the pages are complete, you're ready to upload them to your web host and proceed to the final step—marketing and driving traffic!

But,before you do that, take some time to go through the entire process yourself to make sure that it not only works, but also is clear, and easy to follow.

Drive Traffic to the Squeeze Page

When everything is live online and working properly, it's time to drive traffic. After all, what's the point of having an offer and building a list if no one ever finds it?

To some, the idea of driving traffic is intimidating, but it doesn't have to be difficult. Take a look at this list of options to help get you started, but remember there are plenty of other ways to build traffic, too.

Viral Marketing

Create another free report and link to your squeeze page—and share it everywhere across your social media networks. Get active on Facebook,Twitter, Pinterest, or any other social network where your target audience hangs out.

Don't forget social bookmarking, too. You can also make a video and upload it to YouTube, then link to your squeeze page at the end.

Blog Marketing

There are two different ways to utilize blogs. You can start your own and talk about news and information related to your niche and freebie, and you can leave comments on related blogs in your niche, with a link back to your squeeze page in the URL field of the comment. Both of these are worth trying and can yield excellent results.

Forum Marketing

Remember how we talked about using forums to research for your freebie?

Go back to those forums and start getting involved! Don't just blatantly self promote all the time.

Offer help to the other members—ask and answer questions, and submerse yourself within the topics. You'll become a trusted source of information!

If the forum allows, you can also insert a link to your squeeze page in your forum signature.

Solo Advertisements and Ad Swaps

Solo advertisements require a bit of money to invest, but if you have it, they can work wonders.

This tactic involves paying someone who has a decent sized email list to send a message advertising your deal to all of his or her subscribers. You should expect to pay anywhere from $50 to $100 for this type of ad, but reliable sources will guarantee a certain number of clicks in exchange for this investment.

This method allows you to create an instantaneous burst of traffic to the page, and start getting subscribers within minutes of the ad being sent out.

If you are monetizing your list building—we talked about this in the earlier pages of this report—then you may even start to see some income and cover the cost of the advertisement and possibly even break into generating profit.

If you find yourself low on investment capital, try an ad swap. Find someone who will advertise your list in exchange for you promoting his or her offer.

This will only work once you've got a small list build up—so you may need to do a solo ad to get the ball rolling before this tactic will work.

There are many factors that play into your success with both of these tactics:

☐ ☐ The other person's list will need to contain people interested in your offer. If you're in the dog-training niche, don't buy a solo ad from someone in the weight loss niche.

☐ ☐ Make sure the person has a quality list. Find out how the people became subscribers in the first place, where they came from, and the things they are interested in.

☐ ☐ If you're doing an ad swap, find someone who has a list about the same size as yours.

A R Hipkins

Putting It All Together

If you are truly serious about building a successful online business, you must build an email list. I hope this report has given you a basic understanding of the steps involved in the process so you can start taking action today.

Your email list will allow you to create repeat customers—the best kind— and will strengthen your business through relationship building—turning your business into one people trust and will recommend.

With trust, you will have the ability to sell the more expensive products more easily.

With effective "bait" or something of value for your consumers offered to them for free, you will be successful with your list building efforts.

For the best results, the freebie you offer needs to be something customers really want, and something that truly helps them.

Best of luck to you in your list building efforts!

www.ingramcontent.com/pod-product-compliance
Lightning Source LLC
Chambersburg PA
CBHW051819170526
45167CB00005B/2081